Conquering the Artists Struggle
The art of finding and enjoying your journey

to Jennifer

enjoy the Journey

Silvia

1

Conquering the Artists Struggle
The art of finding and enjoying your journey
Stephen Silver

Silvertoons inc,
2014

First Printing: November 2014

ISBN-13:
978-1502860989

ISBN-10:
1502860988

Silvertoons,Inc
Simi Valley, Ca 93063

818-773-2440

www.silvertoons.com

www.info@silverdrawingacademy.com

Ordering Information:

Special discounts are available on quantity purchases by corporations, associations, educators, and others. For details, contact the publisher at the above listed address.

U.S. trade bookstores and wholesalers: Please contact Silvertoons inc, Tel: (818) 773-2440; or email Silvertoons@yahoo.com

Acknowledgements

I would like to thank the many teachers I have had in my life. My teachers have been family, friends, colleagues, celebrities, writers, musicians, artists, animals, nature and people that I have observed in all facets of life. Most of all I would like to thank my wife Heidi for being so supportive of my path. Organization is one of the key ingredients to life and Heidi keeps my creative brain organized and grounded. My son Caiden, who reminds me of how easy it is to imagine. My daughter Macey, the free spirit that reminds me how to try anything.

Introduction

"Life can't be 100% fulfillment all the time, it is a series of fulfillments throughout the many stages you will encounter along your journey." - Silver

My artistic journey has been a series of obstacles, triumphs, rejections, risk, experimentation, trial and error, rights and wrongs, and ups and downs. It is a journey that we will all experience, but all in a different way.

I left my childhood country and home at the age of ten, emigrating from England to America. I recall leaving behind everything that had been meaningful to me up until that point; friends, family, toys, and even our family cat. My parents told me we were doing this so that my siblings and I could have more opportunities that we may not have had living in England.

In high school I ranked 19th for newspaper cartoonist, out of 19 schools that entered the competition. I was advised numerous times to find a career in architecture if I wanted to make a living as an artist. I was fired from three non-art-related daytime jobs. I dropped out of Junior College at the age of 18. I was told by my parents that if I thought I could make it as an artist without a college degree, then I would have to move out of the house, and pay for my own apartment, car insurance and health insurance. I said, "No problem," and that was the day my life's journey of constantly chasing my desires began.

I tried anything; posting art flyers I made in copy centers, painting store windows at Christmas, and, once I was old enough, drawing caricatures in theme parks, restaurants, and bars. I approached retail storeowners asking if they needed a cartoonist. I started my own t-shirt company that went nowhere. I called people, I showed up at places, I wrote letters, I read books on business. I was persistent, and I learned how to take initiative. I was turned down many, many times. All these experiences in my life were the catalyst for my drive - pushing through, finding new paths, drawing *constantly*, and *practicing* drawing non-stop. Through all of these   lessons, one step at a time, I accomplished many great results; working for   some   of the largest art studios in the world, starting my own business in self-publishing, freelance work, app development, creating and building my own school, traveling and teaching all over the world, working full-time from my home studio, creating a wonderful family, having no debt, and even buying a million dollar home. I just wanted to be making my living as an artist. Whatever I set my mind to do, I did, or at the very least, tried. There are no other things I want to do, other than those I am doing or have done. I am living a life of no regrets, and I want to show you my thought process on why and how.

My life has been, and continues to be, a journey of discovery - seeking and fulfilling my purpose. It has become a life of positive outcomes, due to knowing what I really wanted, doing what I wanted, and in turn, being what I wanted to be- a fulfilled artist and teacher. All this has lead to the writings within this book, and why I wanted to create and share these thoughts with you.

I have met numerous artists in my life, many of whom seem to be unfulfilled in their creative journey. I feel it is the same for many professionals. I personally believe that when we start on this path, we have great passion; a burning desire. This is what establishes the goals we want to achieve. These goals may consist of getting that job in the studio, or the project we wanted to do. We may find that once this happens, we become dormant, and stop setting those goals. It then turns into complaints, frustration, and the constant questioning of, "What is it that I really want to do?" This book is a collection of my trials, and personal thoughts about life as an artist. It's also about reminding ourselves of the importance of setting new goals, creating that passion—and vision, and the courage and perseverance to ignite your dreams again. This book is written for you.

Stephen Silver

GO WITH YOUR GUT, OR YOU'LL BE IN A RUT

If an idea keeps buzzing around in your head, don't ignore it. It is happening for a reason and you should act on it, NOW!!! If you don't, that opportunity will pass you by, and you'll find yourself asking once again, "How come things never happen for me?" It is your job, your mission and your purpose to make the things that you want to have happen a reality. GO WITH YOUR GUT, OR YOU'LL BE IN A RUT!

It's all about change

If you're in a place in your mind or in your life that doesn't meet your expectations, and you're not happy with it, then you must change it. That may sound simple in writing, but you need to discover a way to make it happen. I can only say this because throughout my life, this simple concept has always worked. Start off easy. If I didn't like the way a drawing had turned out, I changed it to my liking. If I didn't like a certain type of food, I changed my eating habits to eat what I liked. If I didn't like the way a certain job was going, I either changed the environment I was in, or changed jobs all together. I can go on and on with the concept of change, how important and essential it is. If you're finding yourself in a place you don't wish to be, don't sit around and complain about your situation, CHANGE IT!!!

Nothing but failure

"A negative mental attitude can bring nothing but failure" –
Napoleon Hill

I wanted to start this week off creating great thoughts. This is
key to the success of whatever it is you desire to have happen
in your life. Like Napoleon Hill said, having a negative mental
attitude can bring nothing but failure. You have no chance of
success if you doubt your actions and your intentions. Your
mind will stop you in your tracks every time. It's tough to
always have a positive outlook on every situation, but know
this, if you don't, you will fail at what you do. The one and only
limitation you have as an individual is the one you create in
your own mind. You have the power! Follow your passion. Be
persistent. Live with enthusiasm.

After eight it's too late

One of my greatest fears in life was having kids. I used to worry about things like how I was going to potty train them. Besides that silly thought, many parents had told me, "Your life is going to change forever once you have kids." GULP! It was an extremely hard concept for me to comprehend. What did this mean? Well for those of us with kids, the first thing we realize is that all of the free time we once had is pretty much gone. Although, I must say, having children has been a fantastic experience so far! Watching them evolve from a tiny, crying, pooping baby into who they are today has been a great journey. Years ago, before I had children, I watched an English film called Seven Up/7 Plus Seven. They showed that the first seven years of a child's life are the most impressionable. This is when their personality is formed, any obsessions in life, traumas they may have, the foods they will like and not like, etc., are all learned and formed during the first seven years of life. This always stuck with me. Once I had kids, one of my objectives as a parent was to make the first 7 to 8 years a great childhood experience, teaching my children life lessons. This brings me to a very rewarding moment I had with my eight-year old son at the time, Caiden. We were working on his homework, and in order to try to get him to speed it up a bit, I tried using a little reverse psychology on him. I said, "Oh, you'll never be able to spell that." To my surprise and pure enjoyment he replied out of the blue, "Dad, if you don't believe, you don't succeed." He then proceeded to spell the word correctly. I have never actually quoted those words to him, but I have always encouraged my kids to follow the ideas that I discuss. It was a proud moment for me as a father.

The 3 P's

I was driving yesterday and heard a great concept on the radio. The person called it The Three Ps; "Pay attention on purpose to the present moment." This philosophy can help relieve the stress so many people create unnecessarily. So often people create scenarios and dramas in their head that often don't even exist. I learned a long time ago to stop myself from creating stories that start with "What if...", and replaying outcomes in my head that have not happened yet. The concept of the 3 Ps stayed with me all day. During the afternoon, I met a great man by the name of Roger. He said to me, "Whatever you do, don't have a stroke!" Well, I will certainly agree to that. I then asked him, "What do you think caused your stroke, was it your diet?" He replied, "Not really. It was all the stress I created for myself. That was the main factor. It brought up high blood pressure and everything else." So, follow the three Ps, "Pay attention on purpose to the present moment." Try not to stress. Be present and enjoy.

I got a chair

This past week when I was in New York for the New York Comic-con, I had an experience that brightened my day. This is the story of the power of belief, which I feel is essential in order to set things in motion, and create the things you want to have happen in your life. Things may happen in a day or in a year, but you must feel and believe that they *will* happen. New York Comic-Con, I feel, does things a little unfairly. When you rent a space that is all they give you. No chairs, no tables, just space. In my case, it was $700 for the space. Then I had to pay $100 extra for a table, and if I wanted a simple folding chair, that would be another $100. Ridiculous, right? I thought so too, so I refused to pay the $100 for a chair I couldn't even keep. My plan was, when I got to New York, I would buy one at a store for $15 or so. On the first morning of the convention I walked around New York looking to buy a chair, but had no luck. That didn't stop me, though. I kept believing and telling myself that I will get a chair and there are no worries. To my pure amazement and delight, as I was walking to the convention, laying on the side of the street in front of a trash can was a folding chair! It was pretty beat up, but nonetheless, right there in front of me was the one thing that I wanted - the thing that was consuming my mind. I became so happy that I even had tears in my eyes, because I knew everything was perfect. The moral of this story is if you want something, I mean really want something badly enough, and you focus on it, it will eventually come to you. This has happened to me throughout my life, and this extra little gift is a perfect reminder that this Universe will provide. I got a chair!

SELF DOUBT that causes stress

"Our doubts are traitors and make us lose the good we often might win by fearing to attempt." -Shakespeare

I think self-doubt is one of the greatest causes of stress and non-progression. Not believing in our own abilities creates fear in ourselves, and causes us not to take the first step in accomplishing what we want. Self-doubt is having that lack of confidence to believe in our own ability. Why do we create this pain within our minds? I believe that self-doubt is based on the fact that we have simply not tried. It is the fear of the unknown. We are often caught up and focused on somebody else's belief, an experience they may have had, something we have heard about. Ask yourself, "What is the worst thing that could happen if I try, if I just do it?" I know my journey as an artist has brought a lot of self-doubt about my own abilities along the way. The fear of what other people may think about my work. It is natural to feel self-doubt, but if we could just let go and change our thoughts into positives, relax and accept what is, then we would succeed. Always remember, do what you can do for yourself, because other people don't run your life. You run your life. You are the sole creator of what it is you wish to achieve. You have full control. I love this quote I once read; "You can either sit on the sidelines, or join in the dance." Make the effort to not doubt, release your fear, believe in yourself, avoid the stress, and enjoy all this wonderful life has to offer. Follow your passion, be persistent, and live with enthusiasm.

Make a positive change

If you keep moaning and complaining about all the wrong things that are in your life, and you're not willing to take initiative and do something about it, then it is always going to remain the same, with no exception! Take the bull by the horns! Create a purpose, a goal! Take action and start now!! Don't wait, don't be scared, just make that change!

Am I successful?

Am I successful? This is often a question people feel they need to answer in order to justify their existence. This is one of those questions that people feel they need to live up to. We burden ourselves with the notion of success for the right to tell others. Believing by stating our success it makes us better. This is mainly due to our fear of criticism. There is more to success than your level of social status or monetary wealth. Monetary and social status, I feel can cripple people. Basing ones success on this philosophy loses the focus of the value of life. I feel success is the achievement of an objective or goal, the success of your relationships with friends and loved ones, living your dreams, being happy and content with what your life is at this moment. You can have goals and wants that are achievable in your future, and for this moment, be content with your successes. There is so much to be proud of every day in our own lives – the success of making it through the day, trying something new, being kind to another human. Look at your small successes, don't get caught up in what "society" thinks is success. Over Thanksgiving I was talking with my 77-year-old father. He told me that up until two years ago, he never felt he was successful. He finally came to the realization that success is not a monetary thing; it is a life of decent decisions that makes it enjoyable and happy. He, along with my mother, raised good children, is still happily married, has no enemies, can still hear (even though it is through a hearing device in one ear), can eat whatever he likes, goes on vacations, and is happy to still be ticking. He has a great sense of humor and always has a truly happy grin on his face. My father gave our family opportunities – opportunities to live a great life while believing in his kids and what they wanted to do in their lives. The next day, while watching Oprah, I saw a young woman who had been through the wringer and wound up at Harvard. Through dedication and hard work, she defined success in an authentic way. She said, "Success, if it is real, creates opportunity for other people." So next time your mind is spinning, and you don't feel like you have succeeded, think simply of these words and ask yourself, what have I done in my life, as small as it may be. That is success.

Don't define what you do, enjoy what you do

I used to spend a lot of my mind power trying to define what it is I did as an artist – who I was, what I had to say. Trying to define what type of artist I was did not help in projecting me forward. At some point along the way, I realized I needed to just enjoy what it is I do. I get to draw for a living. It doesn't matter when or where, just the pure joy of being an artist. Knowing that whatever I think of doing or drawing, I simply do it. I now realize that my journey in life is about enjoying the ride. Everything is a journey, a road trip to a destination. There will be good weather and there will be bad. Keep forging ahead, keep the windshield wipers on during the storm, and know that at some point the storm will pass and you will be back on track. I see it as counting down the miles to my destination – every mile gets me that much closer to what it is I truly wish to do on that journey. Pursue IT, whatever IT may be. Enjoy the process, try something new, no need to define what it is you do, JUST ENJOY IT!!

Our 95-year-old grandmothers advice

Yesterday, my wife's grandmother turned 95 years old. Her name is Lee Rocklin and this is her advice on life:

Be Brave
Be Sweet
Be Kind
Be Loving
Be Happy
Laugh at Everything
Keep Smiling
Don't have a chip on your shoulder
Be Giving
Bring Happiness to Others
Keep in contact with the family
Keep every one informed
Make money, enjoy it and save for a rainy day
Work together with your partner
Play it by ear
Add butter to everything!
Eat candy every day!

Like a puzzle

My belief is that in order to be truly content in life, one must have multiple irons in the fire. This will ensure that you are not bored with the one thing you may be doing, or greatly disappointed if another thing doesn't go through. In order to understand this concept, I equate life to being like a puzzle, built from acquiring many pieces, and creating the big picture. There is a saying, "The whole is greater than the sum of its parts." It is important to start acquiring the various parts of the puzzle, little by little, and start to piece them together one by one for the ultimate goal of finishing that puzzle. The real secret is to understand that you can't just complete one puzzle. You must move on to the next one and understand this is what life is, one challenge after the other. This will create excitement and enthusiasm in what it is you do. Create the picture of your choice (your puzzle), be patient, strategize, and create your vision one step at a time. This is a recurring theme in everything you may do, like reading a book, one chapter at a time, finishing that book and moving on to the next one. Playing a video game, completing one level at time and moving on to the next game. TAKE A CHANCE! Start acquiring the pieces of your next puzzle and be sure to enjoy the results. This is what life is all about, embrace it.

Do the things you don't like to do first

"Procrastination is one of the most common and deadliest of diseases and it's toll on success and happiness is heavy." – Wayne Gretzky

I wanted to share a very useful formula that I have adopted into my way of life. Many of us suffer from the "disease of procrastination"– that part of our brain that intentionally puts off doing something that should be done. It can truly stop us from achieving many of our goals. I have found a solution that is quite effective for me. Here it is... do the things in your day that you don't want to do first. Make this a habit, be consistent and you will learn it's power. After you get the things done you least desire, you can do all the things you really want to do. Doing the things you like or want to do becomes your reward. You will feel more accomplished and your motivation will be increased throughout the day. It takes time and practice in order to make this a daily habit. So give it a try, get the things you don't want to do done first, then do all of the other things on your list. You will see that you'll slowly start to accomplish more in your day, and move that much closer to what it is you love.

Don't settle

"The only way to do great work is to love what you do. If you haven't found it yet, keep looking. Don't settle. As with all matters of the heart, you'll know when you find it." -Steve Jobs, CEO of Apple

In addition to knowing and loving what you do, I feel it's equally important to know what it is you *don't* want to do. Those 'don't wants' in life probably add up to less than the amount of fingers on your hands. This leaves everything else in life open to seeking and experimenting. Opportunities will come throughout your life, one by one. If you want them, take them. If not, just keep moving forward. Do not settle.

Success is not the key to happiness

"Success is not the key to happiness. Happiness is the key to success. If you love what you are doing, you will be successful." –Albert Schweitzer

When I break things down, there are three tenets I choose to follow, guiding me to my own happiness;

1) Follow your passion– no excuses, find bits of time to do it!
2) Be persistent– follow through, never give up!
3) Live with enthusiasm– be excited that you are alive and enjoy it! Make it a great week!

Have a goal to reach

"The tragedy in life doesn't lie in not reaching your goal. The tragedy lies in having no goal to reach." -Benjamin Mays

Life's purpose is to grow. Through growth we learn of new ideas, and new ways to achieve the desires we have for our lives. Having goals is essential. It gives us something to focus on, to wish for, to dream about. The most important part of the goal process is to eliminate any self-doubt. Don't let the voice in your head say that it can't be done. Don't worry about what other people will think or say. It is extremely important to write down what you desire, focus on your desires, and believe that they will come. It all starts with your imagination, your ideas. Set them free, create, think of new ways to do things and make it all happen. *Tell* yourself it will, and in time it will. Just remember to eliminate the enemy, I have found the only true way to make things exciting, especially if you're feeling complacent in what you're currently doing, is by setting goals and trying new things. Take 10 minutes RIGHT NOW!!! Write down what it is you truly want, fix it in your head, believe in it.

Every day do something

"Every day do something that will inch you closer to a better tomorrow." -Doug Firebaugh

This is an ideal mindset to have. We all have thoughts and desires for the things we want and would like to be doing. I often get asked, how am I able to do so many things, stay focused, and have time to be a husband and a parent. Well, the answer is in the quote above; every day I do a little bit of something that helps me fill the many buckets of opportunities I have lined up. Think of designing your life like an automotive assembly line. (I am not talking about multi-tasking, because I don't believe in that.) You can only do one thing at a time, unless you are an alien with multiple brains and arms. In an assembly line, there is a beginning and an end to every car produced. Every action is handled one at a time, until the car is fully built. The car then takes its next journey, traveling to a car lot. Once purchased, its next journey begins, which will be different for every car. Think of structuring what it is you want to accomplish, and follow the same proven method as an assembly line. So, do a little bit of something every day that will eventually blossom into the ride of your life.

"Life is what happens to you while your busy making other plans" - John Lennon

While all of us are busy doing something, life does continue to happen, day-by-day, hour-by-hour, minute-by-minute. The biggest lesson that I have learned is even though we are busy, it is still extremely important to enjoy those moments in life. Accept them no matter what the situation, and don't resist what is happening. It actually makes life a lot more real. We all find ourselves in frustrating situations. If you can step back a bit and observe the situation, as if you were someone on the outside watching yourself react, that can really help get you back to the present moment. Give it a try, it really works.

New goals for the New Year

"I cannot give you the formula for success, but I can give you the formula of failure–which is to try to please everybody." – Herbert Swope, Pulitzer Prize Winner

It is a new year, a new start. This is a time to create new goals. Don't worry about whether you are pleasing anyone around you, what other people may think of you, or what they may think about what you're doing or how you're doing it. It is important to stand alone at times. Make decisions for yourself that you know will enhance the quality of your life. Dream big, constantly remind yourself of what it is you want in your life and follow through. Begin today, and write down what you want. Start your sentence with "I am capable of..."

HOW

It is easy for someone to tell you what to do, but the real question is, how? How do you move forward and create the things you want to actually happen in your life? I thought I would take a try at helping guide those of us out there who want this information. This week I want you to write down on index cards each of your desires. One per card. Simply write down "I want to create my own line of T-shirts," or "I want to have my illustrations hanging in ******* gallery," or " I want to work as a designer for ****** studio." The first rule of having what you want is to know what you want. There is no limit, fill out as many cards, clean and clear, nice and bold as you want.

Now that you have written down your goals, the next step is to start looking and searching. This is an important step. Try and talk to as many people as you can, you never know what you will learn. Seek people who are doing what you want to do, see if they have any answers. Yes it is true, you will come across people who simply do not wish to help, because of ego or jealousy, but have no worries, you do not need these people. However, don't try to get other people to find all the answers for you, this takes away from your growth, and is quite frankly, a lazy approach. If you're going to start a venture and be lazy about it, you will never succeed. The greatest resource is the Internet. Narrow down your search and find out as much information as you can. Through this search you will find other answers. Say you're looking to design a t-shirt line – call up a few printers and get insight into the process, look up wholesale t-shirt manufacturers, look into types of places to sell the shirts, research building a website and setting up a store, etc... the more looking and researching you do, the better. Be persistent, have a strong desire, have a strong passion towards what it is you want to do. Don't do anything just because. You must love it, live it, breathe it, and you can succeed at anything.

When you are clear on what you can do

"When you are clear on what you can do, and intend to do, no one can keep you down" –Carlotta Walls LaNier

Don't forget to keep setting up your targets. Have that one thing, or many things, in your sights. Then it's only a matter of time, practice, and effort before you get that bull's eye.

"How can life give you anything if you don't know what you want yourself?"

"How can life give you anything if you don't know what you want yourself?" – Napoleon Hill

"If you want to achieve success, make today the day you stop drifting. Decide upon a definite goal. Write it down. Commit it to memory. Decide exactly how you plan to achieve it. Then begin by putting the plan into action immediately. Your future is what YOU make of it." –Napoleon Hill

The one lesson that I have truly learned and live by, is the one stated above. It is essential to truly define your specific purpose. Know what it is you are aiming for and what you want, it makes the journey a little bit more exciting and gives you a real purpose. Your definite purpose could be that you want to create the best online web-comic on the internet today – and when you define this, it will set ideas into motion and guide you in your actions in order to fulfill your purpose. Try it out, it is going to be a challenge to define this, but it is the key to your success and happiness. Walt Disney defined his purpose, and look what happened.

Peace of mind

"You will never find peace of mind by allowing other people to live your life for you" -Napoleon Hill

I have had many conversations with students about this dilemma. They are constantly being told how they should live their life as an artist, and what they should or shouldn't be doing. Living your life as a commercial artist requires lots of patience and dedication to the art form. There are no shortcuts. Parents, friends, or other family members may feel that they know what is right for you. As young children and adults, it is true, we need this guidance – but there is a point where you need to take control of the wheel on your own, and not seek everyone else's opinion or approval. This can bind you up for many years until the day comes when you choose to set yourself free and unleash your potential. We are all seeking peace of mind, and by allowing yourself to take full control of your actions, you will be sure to find this exciting path of freedom.

The 5 P's

Passion– To do something without being asked, for the pure love of it.

Purpose– To know what it is you are aiming for.

Practice– To work at your craft daily, and to explore.

Patience– To relax, be present, enjoy the process no matter how long it may take.

Persistence– never, ever give up, find new ways, take initiative, follow your heart.

Clear your mind of can't

"Clear your mind of can't." –Samuel Johnson

Every time we convince ourselves that we are no good at something and tell ourselves we can't do it, well we're right. I believe we can do anything, try anything, and accomplish anything. We just need to get in the right frame of mind and see what result comes from our effort. Something is always better than nothing. My challenge to you this week is start that one thing you've been putting off because you have told yourself you won't succeed at it. Anything, just try it. You'll be surprised.

Do your best

"Do your best every day and your life will gradually expand into satisfying fullness." -Horatio W. Dresser, philosopher

My eight year old who is in Cub Scouts right now has also learned this lesson. "DO YOUR BEST" is the Cub Scout motto. It is a reminder that as long as you try and give things your best effort you will succeed. It teaches us that no matter how hard we try to accomplish whatever goal or task we have, as long as we give it a go and try our best, that is what really counts. If you do nothing there will be nothing.

Experience tells you what to do

"Experience tells you what to do; confidence allows you to do it." -Stan Smith, tennis player

One of the biggest parts of growth for me is gaining experience. Getting out there and trying something, anything, that I may not have been that familiar with before. Trying lots of things builds up your experiences, therefore giving you a better understanding of what it is you're involved in. So by having knowledge and experience with something it will truly guide you in what to do. I think the biggest secret lies is something Stan Smith said; "Having the confidence and believing in yourself will allow you to do it." This is often what will stop us in our tracks. We don't know what will happen. Well in this case I will tell you exactly what my dear old dad told me one day. I remember it vividly. I was about 18 years old sitting on the couch in my parents' living room. I was worrying about what would happen if I asked the shopping mall management for something I wanted, as I was drawing caricatures during the Christmas season. I worried about "WHAT IF" they said NO. So my father said, "What's the worst that could happen? What are you afraid of the most?" "Well," I said, "I don't want to drown, and being stabbed wouldn't be that good either." "So," he said, "Well are they going to drown you or stab you?" and I replied "No." So the worst thing that could happen is that they say NO. And he was right. From that point on I would always have the confidence to just try it.

Don't get discouraged

Often times we set in motion the plan we wish to create. We have the vision, but it doesn't go as planned. This is part of life, acceptance of what is. The thing to do is not lose sight of your target, and start writing or creating the next step forward – possibly a new approach. It may take longer than expected, but don't give up, don't get discouraged, or all the effort you have already put into what you want will definitely amount to nothing.

"Please sir, may I have some more!"

What I am about to share, is a letter to myself that I wrote. My mind is in a state of constant discovery and it is exciting.

Discussing life with my kids the other morning on the car ride to school, I came home and went for my morning walk with my dogs. While walking them, I began to think about all the mixed thoughts you are about to read. So I came home and started writing down the thoughts in my head. It is spontaneous and long, but it is my hope that it may answer questions that I think many of us have. I wasn't going to post this and just keep it to myself, but I have received so many personal e-mails from struggling artists that I thought it would be good to share. The true essence of this is about enjoying the moments we are having right now.

"Please sir, may I have some more". This is a line from Oliver Twist, it stuck out to me because I am constantly trying to explore the way our thoughts and our mind works. I stumbled upon the thought, that as humans, we are always searching for more, even when we get what we ask for, we embrace it for a while but then we want something more. Why is this?

Looking at several scenarios and watching the Biography and History channel, I have noticed that the wealthiest people seem to always want more, thus creating and producing more, and receiving it, but many of them seem to still not be satisfied. Why? Is it because of the need for something more?

I realize more often that there is one true thing to plant in our minds and that is to enjoy what we have right now. No matter how much or how little we have. Life is a series of events, and things will happen. I have seen it. Why are there so many divorces? Is it because someone got what they wanted in the beginning and then it didn't go as planned, so now they want something more? What about the job we wanted, that we now have, but now we want something different, something more. Do we spend too much time looking into the window of other people's lives and think to ourselves we want what they have, we need this we need that? Is this just the true nature of mankind and anything else would be fighting it?

True happiness and contentment, I believe, can only be achieved when you truly enjoy what you have right now.
How can this be achieved? How does one relax with their eyes wide open? What is the feeling we think we would get by having more? Is it the exact same feeling we are having now? I think so. Why wouldn't it be? All the things that we have accumulated in our lives, we wanted at some point in the past and now we have. Did it change anything? For a little while.

As an artist, my whole being is the pursuit of bettering my art by experimenting, exploring, understanding, thinking, telling, discovering new answers, looking for more.

Why does it have to take some form of tragedy within a life for us to appreciate what we have? We know life is short, so what's the rush? Before we know it the end is here. Granted yes, money they say can buy you freedom. Does it? Or does it bear more responsibilities, more stress, more drama, and more expenses? If you really want something, why not make a list of everything you think you want or need. I mean everything. See how many of those things, in reality, you can have right now. It may be stating something as simple as, "I want to be outside in the fresh air more often in front of a campfire."

Why are we so competitive with each other? Why does it even matter what someone else is doing? Can't we just do what we do, make our life the best we can make it? Why does it feel good to win something or gain notoriety – why is this

important? What does it mean? We live in a world where, unfortunately, everybody is taking notes off other people's business; you can never be someone else. You can only be you. Why does it matter what other people think? how does that affect you?

Through simple enjoyment of what one has, I believe "MORE," just happens. So why put any crazy thoughts in your head? Thoughts that can drive you nuts. Why create the story of future events that haven't occurred yet? Don't bother unless Doc Brown can make us a time machine and travel into the future. Why even waste that energy in frustration, is it going to solve something? NO, it will only create worry in your head.

Is it the monotony of the 9–5 day job, working five days a week, sometimes more, in the same routine of daily activities that brings us the longing for more? Can it simply be a matter of changing one's daily routine? Maybe we should become more spontaneous. Do things like walk up the side of that mountain you pass by every week. That one you always say, "One day I'm going to climb that," yet never do. I feel I have discovered that it's the same routine, over and over, that creates this need for more. But that routine never ends, you will always be creating a schedule. So how do we change our routine, what do we need to do to make it all fun, new, and right now? Well, I believe spontaneity is the answer.

Those of us with children understand routine to the max, especially bedtime. Yet there is a real beauty in having kids, because in some ways I get to be a kid again. You explore new things, things an adult usually wouldn't have the opportunity to do unless they were with a child. Things such as swinging on a swing in the park, running across the bridge, going down a pole or a slide on a playground set. Finding farting to be so funny, and bodily functions taking on a whole new kind of

humor. Shooting a Nerf gun, walking down the toy aisle in a store, or jumping on a bouncy again until you're exhausted. Playing video games again, and watching movies from when I was a kid – wanting to introduce them to my own kids.

Before you know it, it may be all too late. That longing for more never got you anything that counted. I heard on a show the other day, "You can't take your bags of luggage in the Hearse." The Egyptian kings got nothing in the end but robbed.

HERE TODAY is the title of a Paul McCartney song, written to his dear friend John Lennon after he had passed. Why do we spend so much time reflecting on what was? Can't what was, be right now? Do what you have to do, and enjoy it! This I believe is the key. Live it, feel it. Every action becomes a new memory, so the secret is to create millions of memories not just dozens. And most important is sharing with other people the experiences of it all.

The Hundredth time I am right

"I think and think for months and years. Ninety nine times, the conclusion is false. The Hundredth time I am right." –Albert Einstein

Albert has it right – not everything you do, think, and say is going to be correct at first. But like I teach my kids and students, with practice and effort you will eventually get it right. There's been a lot of discussion around the issue of people sending out many resumes and portfolios, and not getting a response. I believe as long as you persist, and keep planning and thinking, you are bound to hit. It may take months, it may take years, but the true lesson is never give up.

The wishing game

The other night at the dinner table, my son was upset about something, so suggested we play the wishing game. I said, "In the wishing game, you close your eyes for ten seconds, make a wish of how you want to feel, and it will come true. When you open your eyes you are going to be in a crazy mood." The moment my kids opened their eyes I acted crazy, and they started to mimic me and do the same. We proceeded to start wishing for different moods, and it worked every time. The best part was we all had fun, and within a couple of minutes he got himself into a happy mood again. The mind is a powerful tool, and it is proof that you can act how you want to feel. I often talk about how your mind controls how you choose to feel. He then wished for a tank in the back yard that didn't show up, so I told him sometimes those wishes could take a while, but they will come true if that's what you want. I explained this ten-second wish works best with moods and feelings. So I just wanted to share an experience that worked for me, and those of you with kids will understand. So next time it happens to you, try giving the wishing game a whirl.

Don't miss the silver lining

"Too many people miss the silver lining because they're expecting gold"
 -Maurice Setter

It is important from time to time to write down a list of what makes you happy. It will help you appreciate the things you do have, rather than focusing and dwelling on the things you don't have.

Ability, motivation, attitude

"Ability is what you're capable of doing. Motivation determines what you do. Attitude determines how well you do it." -Lou Holtz

The first step to success is knowing what you are good at. We are all good at something, that is a fact. It may be drawing, it may be communication, and it may be building something. The next step that is so vital, but often times the missing link in taking yourself to the next level, is your motivation. This is KEY! In order to be motivated, it is my belief, you must have love for your ability, a true passion. There is nothing that should ever stop you from doing or going after what you love. Motivation comes with a commitment; you must make an effort to build up the power in your mind to be motivated. The last is having the right attitude, another key factor. You must remain positive about successes and failures that are occurring in your daily life. A person who is negative or has a bad attitude is fearful of something. Fear produces stress and anxiety. Think about what you are scared of the next time you are stressed or having anxiety. Are you scared you won't make the deadline to turn in your project? Are you worried someone won't like your drawing? Now, instead of being stressed, prepare yourself for a successful outcome. Be in a positive place, get rid of bad energy so people will want to be around you or help you.

There is a quote I heard that says "ACT HOW YOU WANT TO FEEL." Your attitude is your choice.

Don't die wondering

"Don't die wondering" –Dr. Wayne Dyer

These words from Dr. Wayne Dyer struck me as to why I think I am so motivated, and don't procrastinate. The statement is short and to the point. If you think about it, dream about it, just go ahead and do it, try it. Make some sort of attempt. Don't live your life wondering what could have been. Don't have regrets because you didn't try.

So, if there is anything that you've been putting off, or have been afraid to do or ask, think of this statement. "DON'T DIE WONDERING."

When in doubt, bail out

I feel this quote says a lot, you don't have to be a mountain climber to understand the basic concept. This can apply to any challenge you are facing. Enjoy.

"When in doubt, bail out. That's a good strategy on Everest and on smaller mountains. There's no loss of face or ego in turning around; it's good judgment. If it doesn't look right today, it might tomorrow. Give yourself the opportunity to try in better conditions, rather than force your way up in dangerous conditions."
-Lou Whittaker, mountain climber

Every second counts

Last week my brother was trying to break his 2 year old daughter's fall as she tumbled down the stairs. Within a split second he fell too, and fractured two of his vertebrae. He is still in the hospital recovering, thankfully not paralyzed. He is grateful that he was able to save his daughter's fall, and that he can move his legs. He was grateful that his mind is still working properly. As we talked he said, "Things like this are a constant reminder of how precious every second is. Over 250,000 people died in less than 1 minute in the Haiti earthquake." I have been asked how I stay so positive; it is for these reasons, and an important reminder that every second counts.

Take the shot

"You miss 100 percent of the shots you never take." -Wayne Gretzky.

Every day I think about life, and am inspired by the thought of new adventures, new journeys, and new goals. It is through this that I often come upon great quotes such as this one by Wayne Gretzky. It inspires me and makes me say to myself, how true. You always have to try something, even if it is small. During mealtimes I find myself repeatedly saying the same thing to my son my mother always said to me. "Unless you try it, you won't know if you like it." Through that taste test adventure, I came to love eating many things - shepherd's pie being one of them. My son is still hesitant, but it is the same concept throughout life. Try something new even though you have never done it. See where it can take you. Let it be an adventure, a learning tool so you know whether it was right or wrong. Because, like Wayne Gretzky said, "You miss 100 percent of the shots you never take."

Get rid of your Frustration

"The only time we suffer is when we believe a thought that argues with what is.
All the stress that we feel is caused by arguing with what is." - Byron Katie

I wanted to share a brief story of Non-Resistance, which I feel is essential to one's sanity. When you resist the fact of what is actually happening in your life or situation, it will result in anger, frustration, anxiety and discomfort. This morning we all woke up at around 8:10am, the exact time I am usually loading my kids in the car. School starts at 8:30am. I could of woken up in a panic, started scrambling, rushing, yelling at the kids to hurry up, build up my heart rate for the result that was inevitable, WE WERE GOING TO BE LATE ANYWAY. Instead I chose to not resist what was, and simply accept the fact we overslept and we were now late. SO WHAT! It's not the end of the world. So the result was, we all got up, my wife got the kids dressed, I made their lunch, and we all sat at the table and ate breakfast in a calm, fun manner and went off to school. No madness, no frustration. So whatever you may be dealing with this week, and something you don't favor is actually happening, try not to resist it. Accept it, and you will find an inner peace that will make it all better.

Get the ball rolling

I am a firm believer in pursuing your independence and doing what you want to do. Don't just sit around waiting for someone to grant you a wish or tap you on the shoulder to give you the job of your dreams. Start something on your own that you want to do. Take the first step, create an idea – whether it is making your own greeting cards, children's books, show concepts, licensing ideas, anything. Just get it started and put it into motion. With the Internet today, you can find all the answers you are looking for. Start today!

Opportunity

"Do not wait for an opportunity to be all that you want to be; when an opportunity to be more than you are now is presented and you feel impelled toward it, take it. It will be the first step toward a greater opportunity."
-Wallace D. Wattles

This quote by Wallace D. Wattles opens up clear insight to the importance of keeping your eyes and ears open. There is no sense in sitting around expecting great things to just happen – they will not. Only through your own efforts will better opportunities present themselves. As Wallace stated, the next job may not be the best, but if it seems one step better than the place you're in right now, that is one step closer to the opportunity you really want to make happen for yourself.

Do something new

I was getting ready to write my Monday morning motivation, but before that I was looking at some of my friends' blogs that I haven't seen in a while. I stopped by my friend Justin Ridge's blog http://justinridgeart.com/blog/ and read this gem, which I wanted to share.

It all starts from the minute you wake up. Be sure to be smiling. You're alive.

I've been thinking a lot about how most of us everyday spend so many hours looking/zoning in front of a computer or television screen (like you're doing right now!), and not really getting out and experiencing life and treating our senses to nature and more physical things. I feel like our brains can function more clearly when it's being exposed to new aromas, fresh air, tactile textures, new people, unique forms in nature, etc. As an artist, that's what we draw inspiration from, and thus create from what we know or have experienced. So why not live life more fully? See more things and get out of our bubbles to do something new?

Justin

Talent

"Everybody has talent; it's just a matter of moving around until you've discovered what it is." –George Lucas

This quote has a lot of truth to it. This is all about experimentation, trying new things, discovering your talent. What do you excel at, and most importantly what is it you like to do the most? I have tried many different art career paths, and it was only through that exploration of being uncertain that I truly discovered what it was I liked to do. I do not believe that talent can be forced. I feel it is already within us, and through exploration it will come out.

DARE!

"All glory comes from daring to begin." -William Shakespeare

It is a simple message, yet a profound one. I wanted to put out a challenge to you this week. Dare to do something that you have been wanting to do. Get it started. It could be joining the gym, making that phone call, or starting a book or project you have been putting off. Make it happen!

Preparation meets opportunity

Preparation meets opportunity. This is a phrase you may have heard before. I have always felt that anything achieved is based on preparation meeting opportunity. Preparation can take hours, days, even years. Opportunity presents itself by keeping your eyes and ears open, and when it comes before you, acting on it. Some people refer to this as luck, when something good or positive happens. I see it as a person's preparation merging with an opportunity at the right time. So, if you want to get "lucky," and do the things you want to do, prepare yourself and keep an eye out and ear open for the opportunity you want.

Believe in yourself

I received an email last week from a young woman who was so afraid of failure, it was stopping her from progressing. My advice to her would be something like this; Believe in yourself and what you're doing, and do not worry what others think. Don't get down on yourself if you aren't exactly where you want to be. I feel it's important to understand that you are in the place that you need to be right now. Becoming successful at anything requires experience, time and practice. You need to go out there, do what you want to do, and do your best.

Press on

"Nothing in the world can take the place of persistence. Talent will not; nothing is more common than unsuccessful men with talent. Genius will not; unrewarded genius is almost a proverb. Education will not; the world is full of educated derelicts. Persistence and determination alone are omnipotent. The slogan 'Press On' has solved and always will solve the problems of the human race." –Calvin Coolidge, 30th President of US (1872 – 1933)

I wanted to share this quote with you because of the importance of one word, "Persistence." We all have a burning desire to do things in our lives but may be afraid, unsure or just lazy. I have found throughout my career that all I have achieved, whether it be finding work, selling books, or getting the things I want in life, have all come through my determination and persistence. By following through and finishing what I start, I achieve one goal at a time. It is time to act! Stop talking about the things you want to do, and start doing them. It is time to press on and start today, to make things happen for your tomorrow.

Above the ground

Last week I had an amazing experience. I am part of an organization called the National Cartoonist Society (NCS). Since 2005, Jeff Bacon, a retired Navy veteran and fellow NCS member, has organized groups of cartoonists to volunteer their time to draw retired and wounded soldiers. This includes soldiers currently enlisted, World War II vets, Korean War vets, and Vietnam vets, all of whom have fought so bravely for our country. The program has gone over so well with the men and women of our military, that the USO now sponsors it.

Last week I was able to go to San Diego with a group of eight artists to draw soldiers for two days. The first day we went to the Naval Hospital. As I was sitting, drawing, and talking with the wounded soldiers being fitted for prosthetic legs, I was once again shown the importance of being grateful, and appreciating every day.

These soldiers had such positive attitudes and smiles on their faces – they were just happy to be alive and above the ground, as they spoke lovingly of their fallen comrades. For me, seeing something like this had a profound impact. It is one thing to sit and watch it on TV, but to talk directly with these guys is something different.

The following day we were flown by helicopter to the USS Bonhomme Richard, a carrier in the middle of the ocean. We were given a tour, and drew as many troops as we could. They were having so much fun, and were just so excited to have us on board. These men and women were getting ready to be deployed for seven months. As I spoke to individuals, I found some who were ready for action, and others who didn't really want to go and be away from their families for so long. Still

others told me they were running away. The captain of the ship spoke to us with confidence, as he talked of his ship and crew. When we asked about his own family, I could feel the sorrow as he talked of missing his daughter's graduation, and that his whole family wouldn't be together again for another year and a half.

Hearing these stories was a reminder for me to appreciate what it is I do have, and not to focus on the things I don't. This was another reminder for me to be grateful, and to appreciate every day and make it count.

If this reaches anyone who is in the service, I am truly grateful for your service, and I am honored to have spent a couple days with our country's heroes.

Goals are dreams with a deadline –Tony Robbins

This is a phrase that has stuck with me. It makes a lot of sense, and after all, don't we all have those dreams floating around in our heads? I wanted to share a great technique that Tony Robbins wrote about in his book, "Awaken the giant within." He talks about laying out your goals in four parts. Now the most important thing to do here is to actually write these down. NOW! Don't just read it.

The first part is to write down your personal goals, and put a time frame; one year, five years, etc. This is what you want to accomplish for you, such as working out, eating healthier, making more time for the spouse etc.

Second, is to write down your career goals and put a time frame. What do you wish to accomplish for your career, your own business, etc.? Don't forget you need to be writing these down.

Third, are your adventure or toy goals, all the fun things. Make this big – why not? The places you want to travel, the home you want to buy, and the stereo system you have always wanted.

And fourth, are your contribution goals. What things are you going to do to give back somehow, to help other people along their journey?

Every so often you will want to add new ones as you finish the ones you accomplish. This is a great feeling, and writing these down will set your mind at ease, moving you toward the happiness you deserve.

There are no mistakes

"There are no mistakes, only lessons. Growth is a process of trial and error, experimentation. The 'failed' experiments are as much a part of the process as the experiment that ultimately 'works'." -Anonymous

This quote struck me as the ultimate truth. This past week I have been pursuing something completely new to me. My brother and I have been working with high-end video camera equipment and editing software. Every time we thought we had figured things out, a new problem arose. Sure it was frustrating, but through each problem I realized it was a lesson. We learned what not to do, and searched for new answers and outcomes. I truly believe that everything happens for a reason, and to never quit! Just try a different approach. Ultimately we figured things out. With this attitude I know there will be a positive outcome. So if something doesn't seem fair, or something has gone wrong, don't let it take you down an empty road. It is not a failure, but a learning experience. Pick yourself up, and believe that you will figure it out and carry on.

Treat life as a journey

Treat life as a journey to your favorite vacation spot. Whenever I am heading somewhere, whether it be a convention, a lecture, or a vacation, (all of which I enjoy), I want and need to know two things; Where am I going, and how am I going to get there? If I'm driving, I may map it out through Yahoo Maps, or punch it into my navigation system – then I am on my way. Once I arrive I feel great, and enjoy the days or weeks I'm there. At some point, I have that urge to come back home. Once I get home, I start to plan the next destination.

This is exactly the same sort of philosophy I have chosen to have in life. It always creates excitement and makes every day of my existence that much greater. In other words, as I have mentioned it before, set new goals (your destination), make a plan on how to achieve your goal (transportation), and once you're there, enjoy your accomplishment (vacation). Once you achieve that goal, then create a new one (your next vacation spot). To me, this is what the beauty of life is all about. The themes are constant.

Create new goals, set new targets, explore new ideas. Staying in one spot for too long can get boring. We have all experienced this going on a vacation and being there for a bit too long. So try this with your career, in your relationships, and look forward to where it will take you. Ignite that fire.

There are no shortcuts

Yesterday morning I found myself thoroughly entertained as I was watching an infomercial. I couldn't break myself away from it and thought to myself, *who watches these things*? Me. *Who believes these things?* Definitely not me. The infomercial was about *Shortcuts to making Millions*. It was one of the funniest things I have ever seen. The guy must have spent a fortune putting this hoax together. What I have come to learn throughout my career, and what I have learned from reading about other people and watching their biographies is, THERE ARE NO SHORTCUTS.

In order to be successful at anything; drawing, painting, sports, cooking, acting, you name it, it simply takes time, effort and determination. I have had many young artists come to me and ask, "How do I get better?" I tell them to draw a lot, explore, and practice. I often get blank stares, and the next question, "Well, what's the secret to *drawing* better?" The answer is the same, draw a lot, explore, and practice. There are no shortcuts. In life, if you enjoy what it is you are doing, you will excel. Your passion is what will drive you to succeed in whatever it is you wish to do. And simply remember...THERE ARE NO SHORTCUTS!

Make every day count

Last week I was at Boy Scout camp with my 7-year-old son, and one afternoon they had an animal show. Every time they brought out an animal, they told us their life expectancy. They ranged from only 3 years for a possum, to 300 years for an alligator. Animals are completely unaware of how long they have to live. During their life, they have to find food, shelter, and a mate. They live a simple life; it is a lot less complicated than ours.

It made me think, as humans, we are fully aware of our time here. It got me thinking about how many days the average person lives. I found out that in the United States, and throughout all western civilized countries, our natural life expectancy is about 80 years. Broken down into days that only gives us about 29,200 days.

To put this into perspective, if you were to tell someone living in the U.S today that throughout their lifetime, they were only going to earn $29,200, they may think to themselves how little money that is. So the point is, we actually have very little time on this earth. Try to MAKE EVERY DAY COUNT, MAKE YOUR GOALS AND DREAMS COME TRUE, KEEP IT SIMPLE, BE GRATEFUL, LIVE YOUR BEST LIFE, SMILE, AND HAVE FUN.

Life

Ed McMahon, Farrah Fawcett, Michael Jackson, Billy Mays, and Chava Pelleg, all lost their lives this past week. Who is Chava Pelleg? She was a dear family friend that also passed away this week. She was no different than any of the others. They all woke up every day, had dreams, visions and aspirations in life, but their lives were cut short. Whether someone is famous or not, everyone has something to share and give. When hearing about someone's death it reminds me of how short our time on earth is. While we are alive, we can do our best to enjoy every minute of every day. Appreciate life. Be thankful, be grateful. Don't sweat the small stuff. Do the things you want to do. Travel, explore, and create. And most importantly, have fun!

Don't get discouraged

"One of the things I learned the hard way was that it doesn't pay to get discouraged. Keeping busy and making optimism a way of life can restore your faith in yourself." –Lucille Ball

When I read this quote, I thought to myself *I learned this very lesson, too*. There was a point in my life when I was drawing caricatures in theme parks, and put myself down a lot. I wanted to be better at drawing, and didn't really know what direction I wanted to take in life. One day, I made the decision to get busy and start learning how to draw. I decided to take a life-drawing class, as well as study some of the great artists. When I started to believe in myself, I realized that I could accomplish anything I set my mind to. It has been a way of life for me ever since.

So keep busy, keep practicing, stay positive, and enjoy every moment.

Looking beyond what you already know

Last week I attended the Annual Licensing Expo in Las Vegas. The Licensing Expo was a big awakening for me, as I saw the potential for many other great ventures. We live in a global market, and with the power of the Internet, many opportunities await us. I feel it is extremely important to look beyond what you already know. It is an essential part of growth. I have mentioned before, in order to break out of the monotony in one's life, you must recharge from time to time. Set new goals; create new targets to aim for. I have been working in the animation industry for over 17 years and know that it is not the end all be all for me. There are so many opportunities out there waiting for us to grab and veer our attention towards. So take the time to go above and beyond to explore, and look ahead of what you already know.

A great quote

I came across this quote and wanted to share. It represents a thought I have had for a while now.

"Don't create the story of a future event. Today is the tomorrow that you worried about yesterday, and all is well." – Anonymous

The voice in your head

I wanted to mention the importance of reminding yourself daily to stay focused and present with what it is you are actually doing at that moment. I feel if you don't do this, you will not be able to train your mind, and the same issues will keep resurfacing. Last week, my mind was starting to wander, and I was getting anxious and frustrated with all the work I had to do. I then walked over to a pad of paper, wrote down my list for that day and week, and told myself I am just working on this specific task right now. I happened to be packing books to send off, so I just focused on that. I also started to sing, which helps me to be present – so I wasn't thinking of all the future stuff I'd have to get to shortly. Stay focused on your present action; you will also do it more efficiently. All these actions put my mind at ease again, and made me really happy. So do whatever you need to do to remind yourself of the present moment on a daily basis. It will make your day go by with ease.

Motivation

"People who are unable to motivate themselves must be content with mediocrity, no matter how impressive their other talents." -Andrew Carnegie

This is a harsh quote, but very true. As a teacher, I have come across many students who wish to succeed in their field, but lack the motivation. Becoming good at anything requires practice and effort and taking the initiative. By working hard outside of a given assignment, it is my belief that those are the individuals who will break through. I have some students now who bring me their artwork that they did during the week that I didn't assign. That is motivation. Don't talk about it- Just do it!

If you can imagine it

"If you can imagine it, you can achieve it; if you can dream it, you can become it." -William Arthur Ward

This quote made me think about kids. They always seem to be ambitious, have great imaginations and dreams. They get a thought in their head, and unless someone stops them, they just go for it. It is great to observe. Set aside some time this week to do what you want to do, use your imagination, and follow your dreams.

Means to an end

Throughout the years there is something that I have actively tried to overcome; and that is not treating everything I do as a means to an end, and embracing and enjoying the means.

I know you have gone through this too. I found that I would be working on something, as we do in production or anything else for that matter, with the mindset of just trying to end it – not really focusing and concentrating on the task at hand. My mind would hop skip and jump, thinking about all the other things I needed to get done, instead of being aware and focused on what it was I was actually doing. It would make the situation somewhat overwhelming and frustrating. This also happened with my kids, focusing on the next thing I had to do, as opposed to just focusing on them at that moment. This would cause me to lose my patience with them. My thoughts were taking me somewhere else. Through that I realized I wasn't doing things as efficiently as I could, and it had to change. Once I came to the realization of needing to be present, and not treating everything as a means to an end, I actively began to make a daily practice out of it. It helped me relax more and enjoy what it was that I was doing at that moment.

I started to apply this simple philosophy with small things on a daily basis, such as washing the dishes, vacuuming, etc., and they all have become relaxing actions to me. Knowing that this is what I am doing at that moment, and I will do my other tasks when I am done with that one. This has helped me a lot with my art. By just enjoying what I am doing at that present moment, knowing it needs to be done and relaxing while doing it. Not treating it as a means to an end, because as long as you are living, there is no end. So enjoy the moment.

Do it for yourself

For many years as an artist I struggled with the fact that I didn't draw as well as my influences, or other artists that I thought had superior talent. I was comparing myself to these artists, which caused this competition within my own head, because my work was not as good as theirs. I questioned my level of talent, which would cause me great frustration. I get emails from people who struggle with this all the time, and they too create their own competition and frustration.

Throughout the years I have learned to be inspired by others work instead of intimidated by it. My philosophy is that I do not have to *be* the best; I just have to *do* my best.

Wallace Wattles had a great quote. He said, "Do not be competitive, be creative." Don't waste your time looking at what the competition is doing – create something new. Look at *your* goals, *your* interests, *your* abilities, rather than the goals, interests, and abilities of others. Do it for yourself!

All you have to do is ask

Being a father of two young children, ages 4 and 6, I am constantly bombarded with them asking me questions of whether or not they can have something or do something. Sometimes they get a yes, sometimes they get a no. But one thing is certain, if they didn't ask, then I wouldn't know what was on their little minds, and they probably wouldn't get what they were wanting either.

This is something that I have found to be extremely important as an adult. If you don't ask, you don't receive. You could sit around all day getting upset about the things you're not receiving. It could be a day off, a raise, wanting to work from home one day a week, or needing to meet with someone. In any case, all one has to do is ask. The answer may be yes, or it may be no.

This past weekend, a young artist I had never met named Kyle was in my hometown. He had nothing to do, so he shot me an e-mail to see if we could meet. We were able to meet for coffee, and later that night I invited him to my home for dinner. All he had to do was ask. I had a nice time speaking with him, and before he left he gave me a great book that I'm enjoying reading. The way I see it, it was meant to be.

So don't get frustrated or complain about not getting the things you want, simply ask for it. What's the worst thing that can happen?

Staying focused

A great lesson I have learned about staying focused is very simple.
Focus on the work you have to do today, today. "Don't do tomorrow's work today." – Napoleon Hill
Don't do a week's worth of work today. When you finish the tasks, your goals for today, relax! If you try to do too much, you will be doing it inefficiently, and that will result in failure. Stay focused, one thing at a time.

Don't create the story

"Do not anticipate trouble, or worry about what may never happen. Keep in the sunlight." -Benjamin Franklin

This quote says it all. The key is to not create the story. We all do it; we create a situation in our mind and our thoughts that doesn't exist. You can easily build up frustration, anxiety, and stress, all for nothing. This will affect your health. How many times have you created that scenario in your head, all for nothing, and the result turned out fine? Keep your thoughts focused on being positive, and the outcome will become positive. You are the cause, and what you put out is the effect.

Words of wisdom

My Aunty Sara's Recipe for a Good and Long Life.
by Sara Rocklin, age 100

Wake up with a smile.
Plan your day.
If you have a dream, follow it.
Don't ever give up on your dreams.
Always look your best; you never know when you are going to meet someone.
Be the first to say hello to others.
Don't hold anger. Let it go. It takes more energy to be angry then to be happy, so you might as well be happy.
Strive for understanding others.
Assist people who need it, and help people with kindness.
Don't give up on people.
Know your family and enjoy them.
When you work, pay your self first and put the money in the bank. SAVE for a rainy day.
Don't get into debt.
About money -- Make it, enjoy it, save it, and give a little to others.
Enjoy your own surroundings.
Enjoy the simple things of life.
Don't envy your friends.
To have a friend, be a friend.
I hope you have the blessings and love that was given to me all of my life. Thank you my dear family and good friends for all the joy you have given to me.

With love, Aunty Sara

Be grateful today

First off, take a real deep breath, it will help relax you. Make today a great day. You are in control of it. Visualize it being great. Whatever tasks that are ahead of you today, accept the fact that they need to be done, and do them with a smile. Be grateful for all the things that you *do* have, rather than focusing on all the things you don't have. Having these feelings of gratitude make everything in your life feel really good. I was driving in traffic this morning with my windows down and enjoyed the fresh air. Simple things make a huge difference.

Do what you Do

If you're a runner, run
If you're a swimmer, swim
If you're a musician, play
If you're a cook, cook
If you're an artist, create
Do what it is you do, because that is happiness.

Spend a calm Life

"Identify your fear, and you'll be in the clear"

Why is it I cannot succeed?
Is it due to fear of how I am perceived?
Will they like me? Will they not?
Will I be accepted? Will I get that studio spot?

Their art is so much better, how can I compete?
What is it that I need to do? I don't like defeat.
I have an answer, I'd like to share–
It states just how to be aware.

Just be you and I'll be me, this is how it ought to be.
Be creative, don't compete,
And in good time, you'll feel complete.

Discover what it is you fear,
And through this journey it will be clear,
That any obstacle will disappear.

Do not beat up on yourself

I now understand why so many artists cannot appreciate their talents.

Listening to an interview with George Lucas, he said, "I was sad that I never got to see Star Wars." He missed the excitement, the hype. This happened because he created it, and was there during the making of it, but he was in the eye of the storm as everything else around him was happening. He was making bits and pieces, and eventually putting it all together. So having been part of the process from the beginning to end, being so close to it, the impact when seeing something fresh and new was completely gone.

It all made sense to me. So many of us creative's go through the same thing, and this is why, quite often, we are not super excited or thrilled about the art we do. Yet other people react to it positively, and vice versa when we see someone else's art that intrigues us.

I think knowing this will help remind you not to beat up on yourself so much when looking at your own work. Don't be so quick to dismiss when someone says they like what you've done. Embrace it, and enjoy the compliment. There is no reason to make excuses about the work and effort you have put in. Know that *this* is why it is so hard to appreciate the impact of your own work – because you have been there from the beginning. You are almost unable to see it anymore. This is the exact same logic as a surprise – a surprise cannot exist if you are aware of its inception and planning. A true surprise is when you encounter something unexpected for the first time. So the lesson remains – do not beat up on yourself if your own artwork does not excite you. Know that you did your best.

Your day

You are the creator of your day. How do you see it? As relaxing, enjoyable, exciting, a day of anger. It all starts with you, and how you react to the circumstances within it. Once you become aware of what the circumstances of any situation are, only you can make the choice of how you are going to react. The more you can find the love or happiness in any situation, the faster you will learn that those situations will no longer occur, or have the same effect on you.

You have a purpose in this life, but only you can discover it. Ignore other people if they don't agree with what you are doing.

Don't give up

"Small events and choices determine the direction of our lives, just as small helms determine the directions of great ships" – M. Russell Ballard

This quote goes with my philosophy of NEVER GIVING UP. We all have choices, and we can all change our circumstances if that is what we really want to do. It is extremely important, however, to know the direction you wish to go – your purpose. Knowing this will be a driving force to reach that destination. Yes, there are going to be bumps and swells and all kinds of tests. Remember that as long as you have your mindset and don't give up, even after what you believe to be countless failures, you will begin to see that you can achieve what it is you set out to do.

Now it is time to revisit that certain objective you have been trying to accomplish, but gave up on because the result didn't come quickly enough. Take another stab at it. See if you can steer it in another direction, opposite of what you attempted before. Give it a whirl and see what happens.

Failures

"The Road to Success is Paved with Failure"   – English proverb

I was recently in Japan doing a seminar. I find as I do more lectures, I learn something new each time I explain things in different ways. The more I speak, the more I learn to simplify my points in order to get them across.

As I was discussing my journey as an artist, I explained how I have never seen failure as failure in my life. Instead, I see it as a lesson to make sure I don't repeat what I have done. Sometimes 'failure' is even the catalyst for me to completely change direction from what I thought was the right approach. I was trying to think of some sayings to use as the title for this post. For instance, "Failure is the stepping stone to success," or "Failure will lead you to success."   Proverbs that, for whatever reason, are retained in my mind, possibly from a past life. And then a day later, I find this–"The Road to Success is Paved with Failure." While it came out of my head, I realized I have heard this many times in my life, but never really understood what it meant back then, like I do now.

If you accept the fact that there is always going to be some kind of obstacle in your life – maybe the wrong job, the wrong relationship, the wrong friends, the wrong school, the wrong teacher, FOR NOW!! – then you will truly understand the meaning of this phrase and the truth it holds. Yes there are hiccups in life; divorces, deaths, loss of work, rejections, wishes not coming true, phone calls not being returned, not getting accepted for a position or other things you wanted. But the point is, as long as you keep going and keep trying, you will eventually succeed in what it is you truly want to do.

I have had so many failures in my life, but the reality is, many people will never know, nor do they need to know – because I have always prevailed and succeeded in other ways. This is so important to grasp, it will open your eyes and make your life clear. It will give you hope, a vision and a feeling, that you are never alone, and this life is yours. How do you want to live it?

I wanted to share with you a letter that I just received the other day from one of my past students at Schoolism.com. I feel it really illustrates the point of never giving up after what you may think is a failure.

Steve,

We haven't spoken in a while and I never got an opportunity to thank you for everything you've taught me.

I feel your course came right at the right time, right before I took my first Dreamworks story-boarding test, I told all my friends I felt like I 'leveled up' while taking the test, when all the things I learned started to sink in.

And two and a half years later, two tests, a lot of ups and downs, and many many drawings, I am now very happy as a newly hired staff story artist at Dreamworks animation. Life is pretty awesome.

Whenever I slack off I can hear your little voice in my head filling me with motivation. You're a truly inspirational teacher.

Yours,

–Guy Bar'ely

Success

Success, the American dream. But what is it, what does it mean? Why do we wrap our existence around this one word? Does it mean we have made it? But made what? Does it mean we are in a better situation than somebody else? Does it mean we are set for life?

I personally don't think it means any of these things. I believe the true meaning within of the word success, means waking up on any given day with ENTHUSIASM, excited about what that day will bring. We have all felt it at one time or another, so we know what that means – enthusiasm often occurs when you have a plan, a place to go, a person to see, a particular drawing to start or complete. But without having that 'something' that excites you about that day, then you will not experience enthusiasm – you will experience self-doubt, stress, worry, anger, you name it. It may also be a sign that you're involved in the wrong calling in your life. You may be getting those whispers in your head that you need to be doing something else, something more than what it is you are doing right now. It is time for change, and it all starts right here, right now. I've met millionaires who aren't "successful." I've met some of the poorest people in third-world countries who are "successful." How is that possible? Simply because they were enthusiastic, and had the 'happy-line' wrinkles on their face to prove it. Replace the word success with enthusiasm, and you will live and feel the difference. I promise you!

IT'S NEVER TOO LATE

"If you got what it takes you can win, today is your day to begin, don't give up now, don't you quit, today is your day, this is it!"
Shania Twain

Those Lyrics are what pulled Shania out of her depression and creative rut.
They hold great meaning, teaching us the lesson that IT'S NEVER TOO LATE!
By making a commitment, creating the time, taking initiative – we can put the ball in motion, and set a speed we are comfortable with. Today is your day!!!

Why

Why should I draw every day?
It will strengthen your shorthand and observation skills.

Why should I learn from other artists?
It will teach you to observe other shape languages that you may not think of or be aware of. It will teach you new techniques.

Why should I create my own intellectual properties?
It will give you your own voice and will give you a purpose. It will give you opportunities to be seen and it can even earn you extra income.

Why should I learn about the business of art?
It will help you protect yourself, make good decisions, build confidence and teach you how to value what you do.

Why should I set goals?
It will teach you to not procrastinate, give you a focus, a target to acquire. It will give you something to look forward to achieving and will help you discover your true purpose.

Why am I not fulfilling what I desire?
Because you're focusing too much on the how instead of understanding why.

Why do I need to take risks?
It will help you break out of the box, your comfort zone. It will help you discover more about yourself your potential. It will help you avoid regret and will open up many possibilities.

Why do I need to be versatile?
It will give you more opportunities as an artist within the studio and freelance environments.

Why should I stop worrying about my future?
Because everything is going to change and nothing is guaranteed. Set goals and follow them through to the best of your ability. Focus on accomplishing one thing at a time.

Start fresh

"If you want to achieve excellence, you can get there today. As of this second, quit doing less-than-excellent work."
— Thomas Jefferson

It all starts from this point forward. Don't worry about the fact that some projects or events may have not gone the way you were hoping. It is now the past. How can you re-strategize and start fresh and do it even better? There was a quote I wrote on every one of my sketchbooks back in the day. "Excellence is never granted to man, but only as a reward of labor." - Sir Joshua Reynolds

Work hard, work smart, think outside the box, love what you do, and start fresh today.

Enjoy your day

I wanted to share with you some of my philosophies in the art of enjoying yourself. There's nothing worse than being stressed out, so I hope this advice helps. Maybe print it out and hang it on your bathroom mirror. Read it every day – until it becomes second nature, a habit.

The goal in our lives is not for us to be BUSY, but for us to be happy, active and engaged. Enjoy what you are doing.

Today I am going to wake up slowly, and take an extra minute to get out of bed

Today I am going to take a longer shower and really feel the hot water

Today I am going to brush my teeth longer

Today I am going to enjoy whatever it is I am going to eat for breakfast

Today I am going to slowly sip my coffee and taste it as it warms up my body

Today I am going to chew my food longer and appreciate all the tastes and textures

Today I am going to take slower steps as I walk to my car

Today I am going to be patient waiting in any line or traffic, I know I will arrive

Today I am going to say hello or smile at everyone I walk past that I make eye contact with

Today I am going to take many breaks, even if they are for only 3 minutes

Today I am going to pay full attention to anyone that talks to me; my boss, kids, wife, etc.

Today I am going to enjoy whatever it is I am going to eat for lunch

Today I am going to find a quiet spot, close my eyes, take deep breaths, and listen

Today I am going to focus on just one thing at a time
Today I am not going to think about tomorrow
Today I am not going to overreact to any situation that occurs
Today I am going to take my sweet old time
Today I am going to pay some more attention to my pets
Today I am aware that every little thing is going to be alright
Today I am going to enjoy whatever it is I am going to eat for dinner
Today I am going to watch some T.V. or read a book before I go to bed
Today I am going to sit in a hot bath and do nothing for 30 minutes
Today I am going to have a great night's sleep

Oh look, it's today again. Every day is today!

Today don't be BUSY!!!!!!! Be HAPPILY ACTIVELY ENGAGED. Enjoy your day!

The right path

When everything feels in alignment, that is when you know you are following the right path. You are feeling good and relaxed, and your days feel joyful. That is the sign you are where you are supposed to be. It is the sign that the things you are focused on and thinking about are facing the direction and path you must keep following. When you start worrying again, and feel like life is not giving you that same feeling of joy you had, it means you have fallen off the path again. It is not until you get back on track that you will have that feeling again.

You can't control the climate and weather conditions. All you can do is plant a seed and water it. Do your best, and believe in what you are doing.

The greatest challenge we face in life is our unwillingness to take risks, which transition to FEAR. What we define as risk is when we do something that we believe in, but are unaware of what we think the result might be. When we start to analyze all the things that are going to need to be done, we hold ourselves back. But the true gift in life is when we allow ourself to invest in *ourself*. This is always the greatest and most fulfilling reward.

Human thought

Are we making the right choices? Are we doing the right thing? Are we saying what we're supposed to, or are we suffering.

Are there rules and regulations we're supposed to follow every time, or can we free ourself from the fears within our mind?

Is it easier than we make it? Do we just go with the flow? Can we open our eyes to freedom to create and learn and grow?

Once we focus on what we want, just try it, experience it, and see where it may go.

Get excited about creating things– not money.

Create something you're proud of, and it will be followed in success.

People believe that if they are not on the top of their game, that others will look down on them. But everyone knows if they were ever in that place of being on top, they would not want people hurting them either. Bottom line is, everyone is sensitive. Jealousy of another human will never let you appreciate your own existence – and what fun you can have if you allow yourself to just be you.

GOT

You think you want what others Got, and they wish they had what others got, and they wish they had what the others got. But the reality is, what you got is what you got. ENJOY IT.

I believe there are only two choices; you either work for someone else, or you create your own business. A business where you are providing a service for others who find value in what you offer, in order to benefit *their* lives somehow. The question is, what gift is it I offer that holds value? I sing, I write, I draw, I organize, I design furniture, I inspire, I build teams, I paint portraits, I paint landscapes, I, I, I...

1-Determine what it is you can offer.
2-Find the resources that relate to what you do
3-What have you seen, what have you heard? Start acquiring the resources, knowledge, and equipment.
4-As you complete an aspect of it, then move on to the next thing, until you have finished what you set out to do.
5-Then you begin the journey of maintaining what you started
6-After awhile, you start to lose interest and want to do something else. When this happens, start over, and repeat the process: steps 1-6

As long as you are you

Last week I had a conversation, discussing what it is I do, and my approach to life. I decided to explain it in writing as simply as possible. I'm not a poet, but this is what I came up with.

All I have ever done
Is enjoyed what I ever do
My mind was open
My mind was clear
I did not stop to think of fear
I open up my mind
Think of an idea
Put it into action
And see what will appear
It can never be a failure
Because I learned along the way
If I did not succeed
I'll try another day
Stay calm and smile, enjoy the things you do
Life will get much better, as long as you are you

For more information about Stephen Silver

www.silvertoons.com - **Website**
www.silverdrawingacademy.com - **Art school**
www.schoolism.com - **Online art classes**
www.silvertoonsapps.com - **Smart phone apps**

To contact for workshops or lectures, please email info@silverdrawingacademy.com or call 818-773-2440

Follow me @

Facebook.com/stephensilver

Youtube.com/silvertoons